Scientists IN ACTION

ASTRONOMERS IN ACTION

CRABTREE
PUBLISHING COMPANY
WWW.CRABTREEBOOKS.COM

Anne Rooney

Scientists IN ACTION

Author: Anne Rooney

Series research and development: Reagan Miller

Editorial director: Kathy Middleton

Photo research: James Nixon

Editors: Paul Humphrey, James Nixon, Janine Deschenes, Reagan Miller

Proofreader and indexer: Lorna Notsch

Designer: Keith Williams (sprout.uk.com)

Prepress technician: Samara Parent

Print coordinator: Katherine Berti

Illustration: Keith Williams (sprout.uk.com)

Consultant: Brianne Manning

Produced for Crabtree Publishing Company by Discovery Books

Cover image: An amateur astronomer examines the stars in California using a catadioptric telescope

Photographs:

Alamy: cover (Marmaduke St. John); pp. 7 bottom (Francis Specker); 10 (Science Photo Library); 16 right (Dino Fracchia); 18 top (Lucas Vallecillos); 21 top (John Warburton-Lee Photography); 28 (NASA/Joel Kowsky)

NASA: pp. 5, 6 (ESA/Hubble Heritage Team); 11 (ESA); 13 bottom (JPL-Caltech); 15 bottom (JPL-Caltech); 17 (Tiago Campante/Peter Devine); 18 bottom (JPL-Caltech/SwRI/MSSS/Roman Tkachenko); 19 (Ames/JPL-Caltech); 20 (JPL-Caltech); title page left, 22 (STS-116 Shuttle Crew); 24, 25 (Desiree Stover)

Wikimedia: pp. 8 bottom (Kumal); 9 top, title page top right, 9 middle (Rept0n1x); 9 bottom (NASA/JPL-Caltech); 13 top (NASA/Paul E. Alers); 14 (NASA/JPL-Caltech/Wendy Stenzel); 21 bottom (Sarah Elliott); 23 (U.S. Department of Energy); 29 (NASA/MSFC)

All other images from Shutterstock

Library and Archives Canada Cataloguing in Publication

Rooney, Anne, author
Astronomers in action / Anne Rooney.

(Scientists in action)
Includes index.
Issued in print and electronic formats.
ISBN 978-0-7787-4646-1 (hardcover).--
ISBN 978-0-7787-4655-3 (softcover).--
ISBN 978-1-4271-2059-5 (HTML)

1. Astronomy--Juvenile literature. 2. Astronomers--Juvenile literature. I. Title.

QB46.R657 2018 j520 C2017-907809-7
C2017-907810-0

Library of Congress Cataloging-in-Publication Data

Names: Rooney, Anne, author.
Title: Astronomers in action / Anne Rooney.
Description: New York, New York : Crabtree Publishing, [2018] | Series: Scientists in action | Includes and index.
Identifiers: LCCN 2018000100 (print) | LCCN 2018006697 (ebook) | ISBN 9781427120595 (Electronic) | ISBN 9780778746461 (hardcover : alk. paper) | ISBN 9780778746553 (pbk. : alk. paper)
Subjects: LCSH: Astronomy--Juvenile literature. | Astronomers--Juvenile literature.
Classification: LCC QB46 (ebook) | LCC QB46 .R6558 2018 (print) | DDC 520--dc23
LC record available at https://lccn.loc.gov/2018000100

Crabtree Publishing Company
www.crabtreebooks.com 1-800-387-7650

Printed in the U.S.A./052018/CG20180309

Published in Canada
Crabtree Publishing
616 Welland Ave.
St. Catharines, Ontario
L2M 5V6

Published in the United States
Crabtree Publishing
PMB 59051
350 Fifth Avenue, 59th Floor
New York, New York 10118

Published in the United Kingdom
Crabtree Publishing
Maritime House
Basin Road North, Hove
BN41 1WR

Published in Australia
Crabtree Publishing
3 Charles Street
Coburg North
VIC, 3058

CONTENTS

WHAT IS ASTRONOMY?

If you stand in a dark place and look up at the night sky, you might see hundreds of stars. In fact, there are at least 100 billion stars just in our part of the universe. You can also see planets, moons, and other objects.

Space scientists, called astronomers, study all types of objects in space. Astronomy is one of the oldest sciences. People have investigated space objects for thousands of years.

A telescope is a tool that helps astronomers see faraway objects in space, such as other planets. You can use a simple telescope to see space objects, too.

Who Are Astronomers?

Astronomers are scientists who work to understand the universe and everything in it, including Earth. They can study objects in our own **solar system**, such as the Sun (our own star), planets, moons, **comets**, **asteroids**, and **meteoroids**. Or they can study other stars and the farthest corners of space.

In this book, you will learn about how astronomers study space, some of the discoveries they have made, and some of the questions they are still working to answer. You will see how they use scientific practices to investigate space, and hear the stories of working astronomers. Maybe one day you will want to become an astronomer yourself.

Astronomers study the Sun, planets, moons, stars, comets, and even other galaxies.

Everything in the Universe

The universe is all of space. It includes everything that exists. It is so big, we can't see all of it. Astronomers are unsure where, or if, the universe ends. In it, there are hundreds of billions of **galaxies**—huge collections of stars. Our galaxy, the Milky Way, has at least 100 billion stars. Planets are large bodies that **orbit**, or travel around, a star. They can be made of gas, ice, rock, or metal, or combinations of these. There are also many smaller chunks of rock, dust, and ice in the solar system.

Astronaut or Astronomer?

Astronauts travel in space, but most astronomers keep their feet firmly on the ground and study space at a distance. They use telescopes, computers, and other equipment to investigate objects in the sky. Most astronomers use a lot of mathematics and physics to interpret the data they collect. They try to figure out what the data can tell us about the universe. Although astronauts sometimes gather data that astronomers can use, they are very different from astronomers.

ASTRONOMERS AT WORK

Astronomers conduct scientific investigations to explore answers to questions such as:

- How has our solar system developed? Where did the planets and moons come from? What are they made of? What is it like both on and inside them? Why do they move the way they do?
- How do stars form, and how do they die? How do stars differ from each other? Which stars have planets of their own?
- How do galaxies develop and what happens inside them?
- We know the universe is expanding (getting larger)—but how quickly? What was the universe like in the past?
- Is there life beyond Earth?

Types of Astronomers

There are two types of astronomers:

- Observational astronomers use telescopes and other tools to observe, or look at, objects in space. They try to discover the objects that exist in space and what they are like.
- Theoretical astronomers try to explain why objects in space exist and how they behave. Their explanations are called theories. Theoretical astronomers then test the theories using different data.

There is a lot of overlap between the two types. Often, theoretical astronomers work to explain new discoveries made by observational astronomers. And observational astronomers look for **evidence** to support theories suggested by theoretical astronomers.

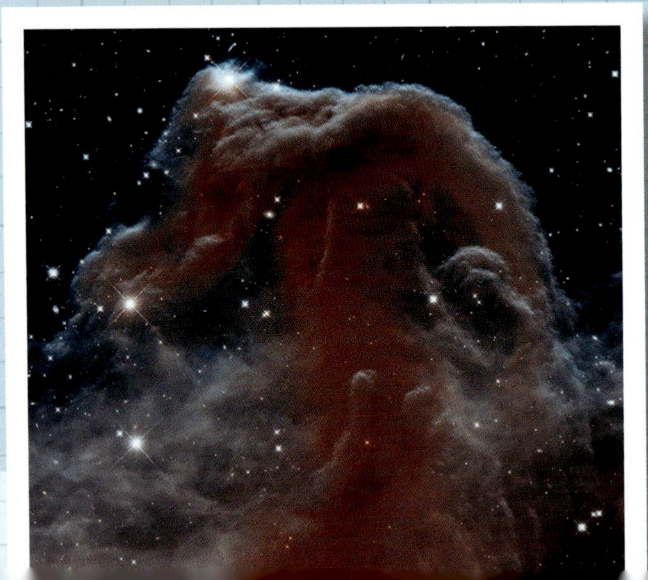

The Horsehead Nebula is an area where new stars are forming.

The Mauna Kea Observatories in Hawaii are very high up, so astronomers can get a particularly clear view of the night sky.

Tools of the Trade

Observational astronomers use a lot of complex equipment to discover the objects that exist far away in space. They might use large telescopes, special cameras, and radio receivers, which use **radio waves** to locate objects. They can also use readings and data collected by and sent from **probes** and **satellites** in space. Most observational astronomers work in **observatories** and at large organizations, such as the National Aeronautics and Space Administration (NASA), Roscosmos (the Russian Space Agency), and the European Space Agency (ESA).

Theoretical astronomers often use the data collected by observational astronomers. They explain and build on the data by using their own knowledge and computer programs to come up with theories and test them. Most work in universities.

You Don't Have to Be a Professional to Be a Star!

Astronomers are not the only people who can observe and explain space objects. Amateur astronomers, or people who practice astronomy as a hobby, can also make important discoveries by observing space using tools, such as telescopes, or interpreting space data. In 2009, an amateur astronomer in Australia noticed a "scar" on the planet Jupiter. It turned out to be a hole in the **atmosphere** caused by an asteroid crashing into the planet. There is more about opportunities for amateur astronomers on page 29.

An amateur astronomer uses a giant telescope at the Mount Wilson Observatory, California.

ASTRONOMY PAST AND PRESENT

The sky has fascinated humans for thousands of years. Some of the oldest structures in the world are lined up with the stars or the rising Sun, showing that our ancestors tracked the movements of space objects.

Astronomy Then and Now

Early astronomers could observe only with the naked eye, but now astronomers use many instruments and even gain information from probes that travel into space. The capabilities and work of astronomers have changed immensely since humans first started tracking the movement of objects in space, at least 12,000 years ago.

Stonehenge is an ancient monument in England. The site is lined up with the rising Sun at particular times of the year.

A sculpture of the astronomer Nicolaus Copernicus in his hometown, Toruń, in Poland.

Earth in Space

For thousands of years, most people thought the Sun and planets traveled around Earth. The Polish astronomer Nicolaus Copernicus suggested in 1543 that Earth and other planets orbit the Sun, but it was another 100 years before this was generally accepted. More huge shifts in our understanding of space happened in the 20th century. In 1927, the Belgian priest Georges Lemaître suggested the universe exploded into being in an instant, rapidly growing to an immense size. In 1929, American astronomer Edwin Hubble showed that there are galaxies beyond our own.

New Ways of Looking

The single most important development in astronomy was the invention of the telescope by Dutch **lensmaker** Hans Lippershey in 1608. For the first time ever, people could see the craters on the Moon. The great Italian scientist Galileo Galilei made a much better telescope and discovered in 1609 that the Milky Way is a band of stars, the planets are other worlds, and that some planets have moons of their own.

Galileo demonstrates his telescope to the doge (ruler) in Venice.

Other new ways of discovering space followed. In the 1850s, chemists found they could tell what stars are made of by examining the light from them. The American radio engineer Karl Jansky discovered radio waves coming from outer space in 1931, and built the first radio telescope to investigate them (see more about radio telescopes on page 16). Today, telescopes based in space, such as the Hubble space telescope (launched in 1990) and the James Webb space telescope (2019), give a crystal clear view of very distant space objects.

Going There

Until the second half of the 20th century, astronomy was carried out from Earth. However, in 1957, the **USSR** launched the first satellite, *Sputnik* (left), into space, and the age of space exploration began. Since the 1960s, the USA, USSR (now Russia), Europe, China, and India have all sent craft to explore moons and planets in the solar system. NASA's *Apollo 11* spacecraft carried the first astronauts to land on the Moon in 1969. The astronauts brought 47 pounds (21 kg) of soil and rock back to Earth for **analysis**.

NASA's Mars ***rover*** Curiosity *studied rocks on the planet's surface in 2012.*

ASTRONOMERS AS SCIENTISTS

All scientists follow careful practices to make sure the data and results they gather are accurate and reliable. This involves asking questions, exploring answers through a variety of methods, using logic and mathematics to examine results, and presenting conclusions that can be supported by evidence.

Scientific Practices

Investigations in science involve the following practices:

- Asking questions
- Developing methods of investigation, including building **models** and designing observations and experiments
- Carrying out investigations
- Analyzing and **interpreting** data collected
- Using mathematics and technology to process data
- Constructing explanations from evidence
- Communicating findings and conclusions

The Search for Answers

Like other scientists, astronomers ask questions and then search for evidence to answer these questions. Usually, they begin by forming a prediction, or **hypothesis**. This is an idea that can be tested by an investigation. For example, an astronomer might look at data that has been collected about a planet and form a hypothesis about the materials the planet is made of. While some scientists can carry out experiments, that is rarely possible for astronomers. They can't set a planet on a new orbit to see how it might move, or create a star to see how it grows.

The Voyager 2 *spacecraft passed near Neptune in 1989 on its long journey to leave the solar system. Astronomers set up the* Voyager *mission with little idea of what it would find.*

Astronomers have two main methods of investigation. They can begin with a very general observation, such as sending a space probe to a planet to see what it can find. Or they can begin with a very precise goal, such as measuring the temperature on a moon or planet.

Making Models

Astronomers often use theoretical and mathematical models. These can be sets of equations that predict such things as how a planet will move in orbit. Or, they can be computer programs that recreate the behavior of objects, such as forming stars. Sometimes, the models can be tested, or proven correct or incorrect, based on the data from new observations. Other times, observations are not possible and they can only be tested with more mathematics.

Problems Are Not Always Bad

A scientific investigation might be straightforward, but often there are problems or surprises. Parts of the investigation might have to be repeated or adapted, or new discoveries might change the course of the investigation. For example, a probe or satellite may get lost or malfunction.

Astronomers must be able to adapt, or change, their investigations when this happens. They share both ideas and difficulties with others, **collaborating** to get the best outcome. Often, setbacks can provide as much valuable information as an investigation that turns out as expected. When a theory proves to be wrong, it can be helpful to astronomers because they can change directions and pursue new theories.

As part of the Rosetta *mission in 2014, the* Philae ***lander*** *crash-landed on the comet it was visiting. Despite it landing in the wrong place, astronomers were still able to analyze the data it sent back.*

Sharing and Moving On

After an investigation, astronomers need to process the data gathered, analyze whether the results support their hypothesis, and draw their conclusions. To process data means to analyze it to come up with meaningful patterns or information. Finally, they communicate their findings, methods, and conclusions to other scientists. In this way, their work becomes useful to the wider scientific community and contributes to progress in their field.

ASKING QUESTIONS

Scientists begin every investigation by asking one or more questions. These can have a broad focus, such as "How was the solar system formed?" or a very narrow focus, such as "How hot is the planet Venus?" Questions can come from existing research findings, from new observations, and from natural events such as an eclipse or the passing of a comet.

A total solar eclipse gives astronomers a valuable opportunity to study the Sun. A total eclipse occurs when the Sun is blocked completely by the moon, as seen on Earth. A partial eclipse is when some of the Sun is blocked by the moon.

Making the Most of Events

We can't make an astronomical event happen, so astronomers make the most of one when it does occur, such as a close approach to a planet.

An eclipse happens when the moon passes between the Sun and Earth, blotting out the Sun as seen from Earth. On August 21, 2017, a total eclipse was visible from North America—you might have seen it. Astronomers used the chance to try out new techniques and explore several questions. One was, "Why is the corona (the outer part of the Sun's atmosphere) so much hotter than its surface?" The corona cannot be seen in bright daylight, but it could be observed during the eclipse. The eclipse made the planet Mercury more visible, too, so astronomers also took the chance to investigate its surface.

From the Field: Dr. Madhulika Guhathakurta

Dr. Madhulika Guhathakurta was NASA's lead scientist monitoring the 2017 total eclipse. Born in India, she earned a master's degree in **astrophysics** in Delhi and a doctorate (PhD) in physics in Boulder, Colorado. Her expertise is understanding the Sun's corona and weather systems. She aims to find out how the Sun's weather works so that she can predict its impact on Earth.

Broad and Narrow Questions

Many of the broad questions that astronomers ask are too large to tackle with a single investigation. Answers are pieced together from many smaller investigations. For example, by investigating the materials that make up asteroids and comets, astronomers learn about the materials that formed the planets.

The observations that come from broad investigations often lead astronomers to more focused work. Around the world, more than 100 radio telescopes monitor signals reaching Earth from space. The telescopes are set up to record all data coming from space, so astronomers can see what exists and happens there. Astronomers sift through the data, looking for anything interesting. Questions emerge from looking at this kind of raw, or unedited, data, and new projects are set up to investigate details.

Some astronomers conduct investigations to find out how families of asteroids are created.

STARTING AN INVESTIGATION

A new investigation can emerge, or come, from previous research, observations, or theoretical models. For example, the search for the existence of **exoplanets**, or planets that exist outside our solar system, began from existing observations that many other stars like our Sun exist. Astronomers started the investigation by asking the question: If there are other stars like ours, might they also have similar planets?

The Kepler Mission

The Kepler Mission is an investigation that looks for exoplanets. It grew out of work by American astronomer William Borucki, who became the principal, or lead, investigator of the mission. In 1971, Borucki suggested a way that astronomers could discover new exoplanets (see page 16). He realized in 1984 that to find planets the size of Earth, a telescope would have to be sent into space. Borucki began to promote and develop the mission that would finally be launched in 2009.

The Kepler *space observatory in orbit around Earth. It was launched by NASA to search for exoplanets.*

Kepler's Questions

Kepler Mission scientists set out to answer a few questions: How many Earth-size exoplanets are in our galaxy? In particular, how many exist in the habitable zones (right) of solar systems like ours? Astronomers used the space telescope to observe a specific area of our galaxy, the Milky Way, to answer these questions and collect data on:

- the number of exoplanets in or near the habitable zone of a star
- the sizes and shapes of the exoplanets' orbits
- features of exoplanets of different sizes and types (are they made of rock or gas, for example?)
- the features, such as sizes and temperatures, of stars that have planetary systems, or planets orbiting them

The astronomers running the Kepler Mission hope to eventually calculate how many stars in the galaxy might have Earth-like, habitable planets orbiting them.

The habitable zone around a star is the region in which planets might have liquid water and so could possibly support life.

The First Exoplanets

Two radio astronomers, Polish-born Aleksander Wolszczan and Canadian Dale Frail, discovered the first two exoplanets in 1992. Radio astronomers learn about space objects by studying the radio waves and **electromagnetic radiation** coming from them. Working at the Arecibo Observatory in Puerto Rico in 1990, they found a new pulsar. A pulsar is a rapidly rotating neutron star. This is a star that has collapsed at the end of its life. By measuring the time between pulses of radiation coming from the pulsar, they discovered that two planets orbit the pulsar, both about three times the **mass** of Earth.

The first exoplanets were found orbiting a spinning pulsar.

COLLECTING DATA

Astronomers collect data in many different ways. They can use telescopes that magnify faraway objects, but that is not the only way of gathering data from space. Stars and other space objects emit, or give off, many different kinds of electromagnetic radiation. Astronomers can learn about space objects by studying radiation signals coming from space. Radio telescopes “listen” to radio waves from space, and other types of telescopes collect **microwaves** and **X-rays**.

Radio telescopes work in daylight as well as at night, collecting radio data from space.

An astronomer analyzes the data received from a radio telescope.

A New Method

The Kepler Mission required a type of data that had not been collected before, so the astronomers built new equipment and wrote software to manage and process the data.

A specially developed telescope was launched into space and focused on a small area of the Milky Way, which it observed constantly, recording the brightness of stars in that patch. It used a technique called photometry to measure any change in brightness. If an exoplanet in orbit passes in front of a star, it will block some of the star’s light, causing it to dim. Since planets are in regular orbits, the dimming of light will happen at regular intervals, or time periods. The research team had to improve photometry methods, as well as build and test equipment, to accurately record data.

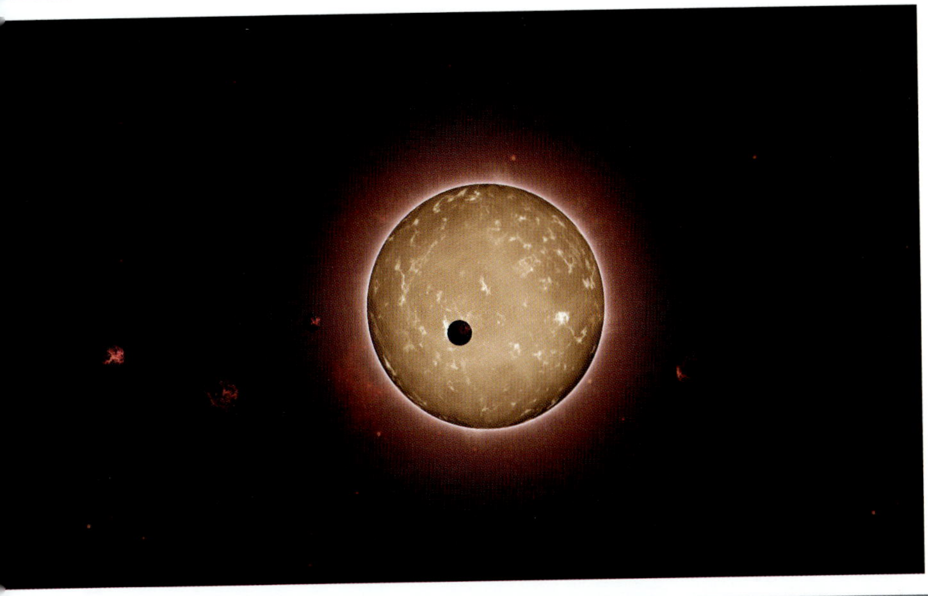

As a planet passes in front of a star, the amount of light coming from the star decreases slightly as part of it is blocked by the planet.

Kepler looked for three instances of dimming at a regular interval to indicate a passing planet. But a star could have more than one planet, so the software also had to take into account several patterns of dimming for each star. Kepler observed 150,000 stars for four years, from 2009 to 2013.

From the Field: Jeff Smith

Jeff Smith is a data scientist working at NASA. He helped develop the software for turning data from Kepler into useful information. The main challenge was to find meaningful dips in the brightness of stars, as the change could be as tiny as 0.002 percent. Once the mission started collecting data, Smith constantly improved the software, perfecting the methods of finding changes in brightness.

Dealing with Data

A project such as the Kepler Mission produces huge amounts of data. The data is first processed by computers, which scanned the records of each star's brightness looking for evidence of dimming. Any stars that showed evidence of dimming were first labelled Kepler Objects of Interest (KOIs). If they passed further tests, this could be evidence that planets orbit them.

WORKING WITH DATA

Some investigations begin with unexplained data gathered by telescopes, probes, or landers. In other cases, astronomers collect the data needed to try to answer a question. The collected data is then processed, or analyzed, to draw conclusions about what it means.

Astronomers spend a lot of time working with computers, analyzing the data they receive.

Jupiter's Great Spots

Astronomers have seen "Great Spots" on Jupiter since the invention of the telescope. Improved telescopes revealed that the spots are giant storms. But astronomers could only investigate them properly once they could send probes close to Jupiter, which would take photographs and make measurements. Images from NASA's *Juno* mission, which is a probe sent to investigate Jupiter and its moons, provide an overwhelming amount of data. The raw, or unedited, images were put online at the JunoCam website for citizen scientists—members of the public with an interest in aiding and advancing a scientific field—to process and find interesting features. In this way, NASA can use the goodwill and expertise of more people than it could ever employ, and amateur astronomers can get involved in real discoveries.

This image was processed by a citizen scientist to draw the viewer's attention to a giant swirling storm on Jupiter.

Searching Kepler Data

The Kepler Mission collected important data with its space telescope and sent it to computers on Earth. Processing data is a vital part of the work. After computers had identified KOIs, astronomers examined their stars closely to determine whether they actually had planets orbiting them, and what these planets may be like. The data collection part of the mission finished in 2013, but astronomers are still working on processing the data and will do so for many years to come. By the end of 2017, astronomers had identified 2,337 exoplanets from the Kepler data, with another 4,496 potential planets still to investigate.

A size comparison of Earth-like planets discovered by Kepler. Earth is shown on the right. Astronomers don't know what these planets look like, but they have some idea of their composition, or what materials they are made of.

From the Field: Helen Giles

While completing a degree in astrophysics, Helen Giles worked as an intern at the university in Pasadena, California, searching the Kepler data for planets with long orbits. Her team found an exoplanet that takes nearly three years to orbit its star. Inspired to work more on exoplanets, she went on to study at the University of Geneva in Switzerland, using data collected by Kepler's K2 mission (see page 25) to look for large exoplanets and to study the magnetic activity of small stars.

SHARING INFORMATION

It is extremely important for scientists to communicate their findings to other scientists in the field and to the general public. When scientists share their findings with each other, the scientific community can build on the work and create new investigations. Sharing findings with the public is also vital to inspire interest in the field and to educate people.

Is It Correct?

Scientists share details of their investigations right from the start. They publish their plans, methods, data, results, and findings in **journals** and share them at **conferences**. When possible, they repeat investigations and compare the results with the original findings. Other scientists working in the same field check methods and results in a process called peer review. They look for mistakes, alternative explanations, and even **fraud**. This helps to make sure results of an investigation are accurate and valid before they are accepted as being true.

Watery Moon

Enceladus is a moon of Saturn, mostly covered by fresh ice. Little was known about it before the *Cassini* spacecraft flew close to it in 2005. *Cassini* collected data about the moon, including patterns of **gravity** and precise measurements of its movement. In 2015, astronomers interpreting the *Cassini* data reported that the moon's slightly wobbly orbit must be caused by a large liquid ocean around 18 to 25 miles (30 to 40 km) beneath the ice. By sharing completed work and work-in-progress, astronomers benefit from insights and suggestions from other scientists. Their own work can then lead to new investigations by other scientists.

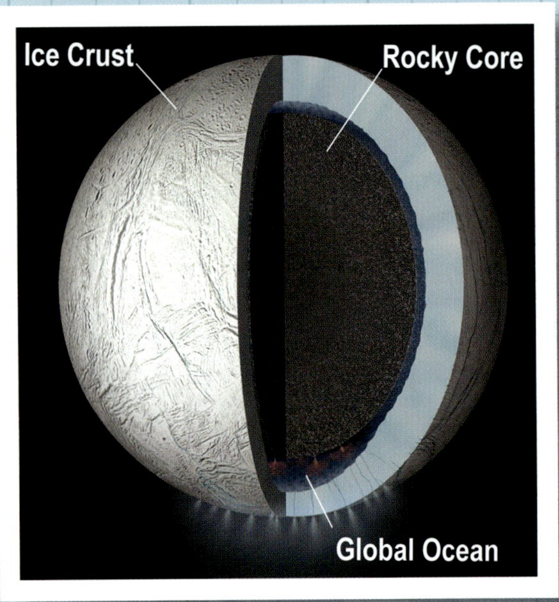

From data collected by Cassini*, astronomers believe Enceladus has an ocean of liquid water beneath its frozen surface.*

Spreading the Word

Scientists also communicate their findings to the public. Science needs new people inspired to take up careers in the subject. It needs engagement from the public, too. Most astronomy research is funded, or paid for, through **taxes**, so it's important to let people see how their money has been spent and encourage them to support the research in the future. Many astronomers work in education and public engagement. They work in museums and **planetariums**, give classes and lectures, write books and magazine articles, contribute to television shows, and work for universities and organizations such as NASA to engage public interest.

Visitors to a planetarium, such as this one in Beijing, China, can learn about space from stunning displays and animations.

From the Field: Neil deGrasse Tyson

Neil deGrasse Tyson is an astronomer who is very involved in public communication. He is director of the Hayden Planetarium in New York City. He gives public lectures, has taught astronomy at Princeton University, and has written many astronomy books and articles. The information he shares is not the result of his own research, but rather the findings of many professional astronomers working over years on many different projects.

Neil deGrasse Tyson has done a lot of work to promote and explain space exploration.

WORKING TOGETHER

Science is a collaborative activity. People work together and share information, including their research findings and problems. In this way, scientists contribute to each other's projects.

Global Effort

Astronomy is an international science. Large projects combine skills from people around the world, and space agencies such as NASA and ESA make their data available to experts internationally. Large telescopes are expensive to build and spacecraft are expensive to launch, so collaboration among countries and organizations is needed to fund these large projects. The International Space Station is funded and run by space agencies around the world. It is used for research by astronomers from many countries.

Astronomers from many countries suggest experiments and investigations to carry out on the International Space Station.

An International Standard: the Metric System

Scientists around the world use the metric system of measurements. Using the same units makes it very easy for astronomers to collaborate and to share and compare results. Metric units are easy to work with, as they are all based on multiples of 10 (for instance, 10 millimeters in a centimeter, 100 centimeters in a meter, 1,000 meters in a kilometer).

New Ideas for Old

An important feature of science is that new evidence can lead to any existing idea being adjusted or rejected. A good scientist does not try to defend a model or idea if something better comes along. In the 1990s, astronomers concluded that the rate at which the universe is expanding is increasing. They suggested an unexplained "dark energy" pushes matter apart. They believed that this energy works against gravity, which pulls it together. But in 2016, new measurements suggested that the rate of expansion is constant—dark energy might not exist after all.

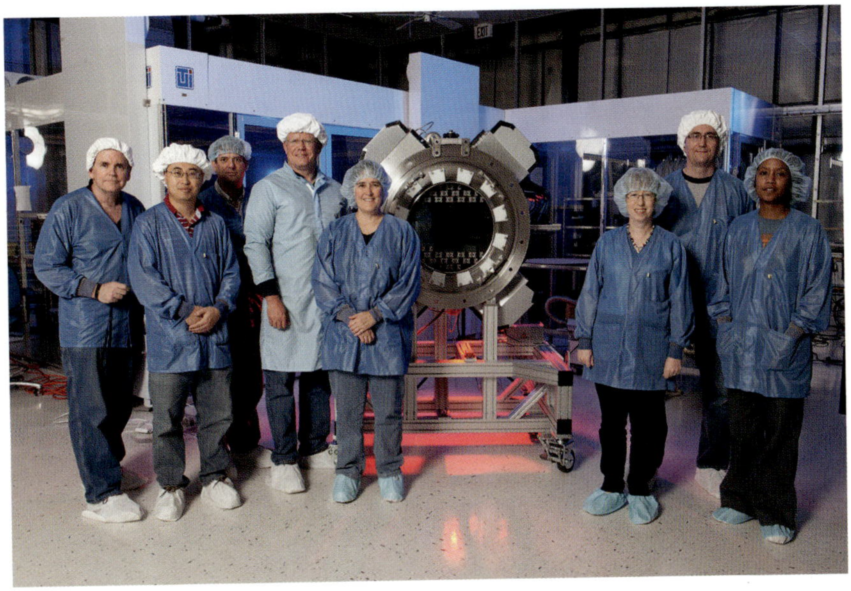

This team of astronomers at the Fermi National Accelerator Laboratory near Chicago, Illinois, is measuring the expansion of the universe and developing better models to explain dark energy.

Astronomer of the Dark

Priyamvada Natarajan is a professor of astronomy and physics at Yale University. She works on dark matter and dark energy, producing maps showing how they are distributed in the universe. No one knows exactly what dark matter and dark energy are. They are terms used for the parts of the universe that we cannot see, but evidence suggests are there. Astronomers know only that we can account for, or explain, just 5 percent of the mass of the universe. This means that there is a lot of something else that we can't see or measure. Part of Natarajan's work is to develop methods that test the models of dark energy that astronomers come up with. She is part of a collaborative effort to learn more about dark matter and dark energy.

SCIENCE GOES ON

The findings of an investigation often lead to new research. An investigation might collect data that needs to be explored further, or techniques or equipment designed for one investigation might have uses for another project. Sometimes, an investigation runs into problems, which are then explored. Missions that don't yield the results expected are often just as valuable to science as those that do.

Magnetic Foam

For decades, astronomers assumed the Sun's magnetic field ended cleanly at the edge of the solar system. But they had to rethink this idea when NASA launched the Voyager Mission. This mission sent twin spacecraft—Voyager 1 and 2, to explore our solar system and beyond. Using data from Voyager 2, astronomers came up with a new model, which has the magnetic field ending in a chaotic foam of "bubbles" of magnetism. The craft will continue to return data about the conditions it finds until the late 2020s.

Instead of neat "folds" at the edge of the Sun's magnetic field (below left), the Voyager 2 spacecraft seems to have found "bubbles" of magnetism (below right).

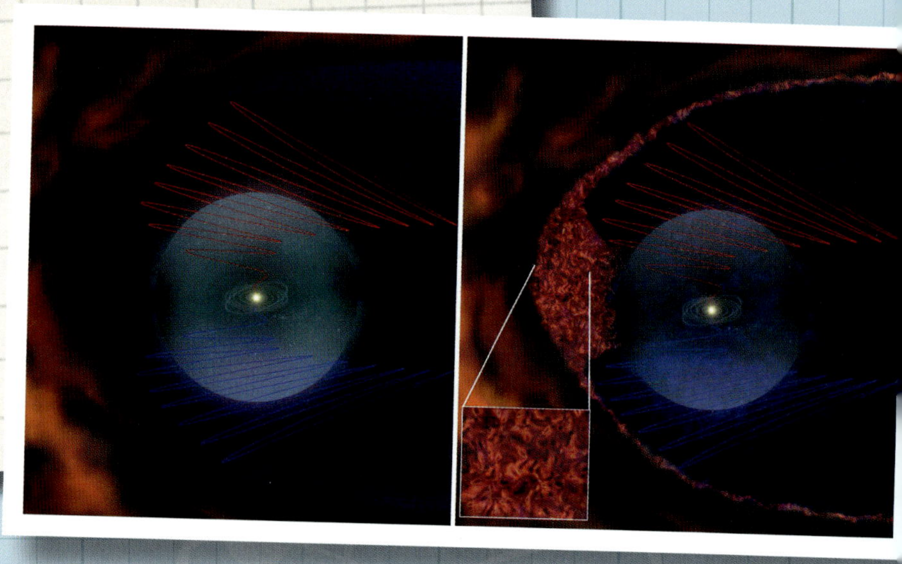

New Life for New Methods

The Kepler Mission has already led to new research. Some of the techniques developed specifically for Kepler, such as photometry, are being adapted for another mission to search for exoplanets with the James Webb space telescope, due for launch in 2019. Jeff Smith (see page 17) is already adapting the software from Kepler to work with the new telescope.

The James Webb space telescope will follow up on Kepler's discoveries by looking for oxygen and other gases on exoplanets. These could signal that life is present there.

Things Go Wrong

The Kepler Mission was cut short because the Kepler space telescope developed a problem that meant it could no longer be held steady enough to hold its focus on a specific portion of sky. Rather than abandon the mission completely, the Kepler team asked other astronomers what useful data Kepler could collect for them. This led to a new mission, called K2. It used the same satellite, but instead of looking at the same patch of sky for a long time, the Kepler telescope focuses on different locations requested by astronomers for much shorter periods.

Although disappointing, the problem taught astronomers a great deal. They carefully analyzed the satellite's failure from the earliest stages. The team looked back through the data to find warning signs of the problem. Now that they know which signs to look for, the team is much better equipped to deal with future missions.

Understanding Limitations

No single investigation will ever discover everything about a topic; it will always need to be followed up by further studies. The Kepler Mission could only detect exoplanets lying between Kepler's line of sight and their star. Most planets will not be in this specific orbit. Imagine astronomers on a distant exoplanet using a similar system. They would have only a 0.47 percent chance of finding Earth!

HANDS-ON INVESTIGATION

You might have noticed that you can see more stars on a very dark night than when there is a full moon or when you are in a well-lit city area. **Light pollution** is a big problem for astronomers. When there are many lights on the ground, it makes the sky brighter and any illuminated space objects, such as stars, look dimmer. This makes it more difficult to view space objects that are not very bright.

Ask a Question

In this investigation, you will set out to answer the question:
How does light pollution affect how many stars I can see?

Develop Equipment

- Wash out a juice carton or plastic bottle.
- Carefully cut the bottom off.
- Tape two pieces of white thread across the open end to form a cross (right). These are cross-hairs that will help you to center the view. Measure carefully to make sure you place them centrally.
- You will look through the opening at the top to use this as your viewer.

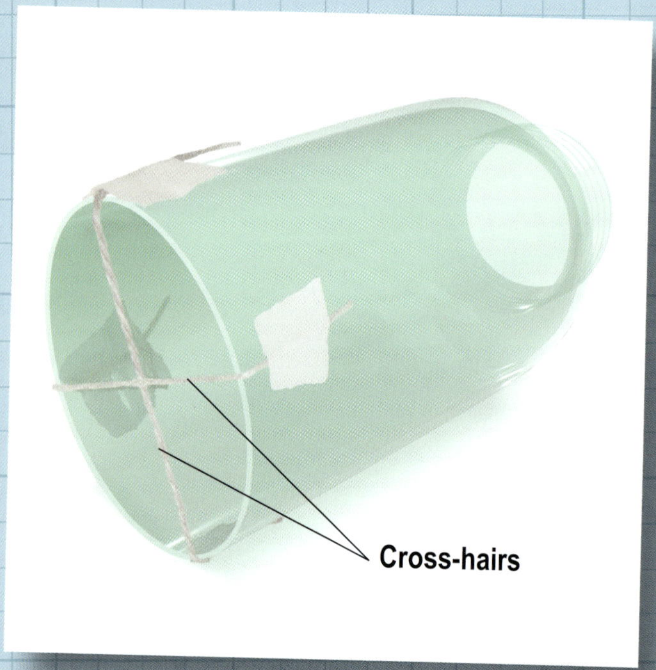

The cross-hairs on your viewer should divide the patch of sky you see into four areas of equal sizes.

Method

You will use your viewer on at least two different nights to count stars. The aim is to count how many stars you can see in different levels of light. You could choose different locations—maybe one in a dark, rural area and one in a town where there is light pollution. Or you could choose a night with a full moon and a night with a new moon. You will need each night to be clear and cloudless, so you might have to wait for the right conditions.

Collecting Data

- On each occasion, you will need to look at the same area of sky. Find a star you can easily locate. You could choose Polaris (the star closest to Earth's North Pole), or a prominent star in a **constellation** you know.
- Center the view on your chosen star, and count how many stars you can see in each of the four areas of sky visible in your viewer.
- For a fair comparison, each time you count stars in your viewer, go out at the same time of night and center the cross-hairs of your viewer on the same star.

You can make as many observations as you like. Try to do this over a relatively short period of time—two or three weeks—so that the light levels do not change much at the time you have chosen.

The North Star (Polaris) is a star that you could choose to focus your viewfinder on.

Observations

You will need to write down your observations as you view the night sky. Remember that your goal is to find out how light pollution affects the number of stars you see. Make a chart that records the date you are viewing and the number of stars you counted on each date.

You could also record the brightness of stars to gather further data about light pollution. Rate the brightness of stars from 1 being least bright to 3 being very bright. Record how many stars of each rating of brightness you see.

Interpreting Data

How will you analyze the data you collect? Perhaps you could calculate the percentage difference in the number of stars you can see each night. Or, you could figure out the average difference in the levels of brightness of the stars each night. Find a good way to present your data. You could use charts, graphs, or diagrams. What conclusions can you draw about how light pollution affects the visibility of the stars?

Explaining and Sharing Findings

Design a poster or presentation to share details of your investigation. Include the question you were addressing and the method you used. Explain how you analyzed the data you collected and reached your conclusions. Could you improve your method if you had more time or resources? If so, how?

Members of the public use telescopes at an astronomy club. Using a telescope would allow you to make even more detailed investigations of the stars.

LOOKING AHEAD

Astronomy will always excite people, and there will always be more for astronomers to discover. Some of the projects just beginning now will still be going years from now, when you could be an astronomer!

Make a Start!

You can make a start by joining an astronomy club—there might be one at your school or a local college. Maybe there's a planetarium, observatory, or space center you could visit, too.

You can even get involved with some real astronomy. For example, NASA runs a yearly astronomy contest for young people. In 2017, contestants looked at images of Saturn taken by the *Cassini* spacecraft and wrote an essay explaining which image they thought would provide the most useful scientific results. You could try something like this with your peers. Sharing and discussing your ideas will give you practice at being part of a scientific community.

NASA's Space Launch System (SLS), still in development, will be the most powerful rocket ever built. Its planned future missions include a visit to an asteroid and to Mars.

Where Are We Going?

Astronomers at NASA will continue to explore the planets and moons of the solar system. In particular, astronomers will search the icy moons orbiting gas giants, or planets made entirely or almost entirely of gas, for signs of past or present life. These moons include Saturn's Enceladus and Jupiter's Europa. NASA plans a Mars landing in the 2030s, too.

LEARNING MORE

BOOKS

Einspruch, Andrew. *Mysteries of the Universe: How Astronomers Explore Space.* National Geographic Children's Books, 2006.

King, Bob. *Night Sky with the Naked Eye.* Page Street Publishing Company, 2016.

Space! Dorling Kindersley/Smithsonian, 2015.

PLACES TO VISIT

A planetarium is a great place to learn about space. You can find one near you here:

USA
www.go-astronomy.com/planetariums.htm

Canada
http://casca.ca/?page_id=451

Check local colleges, universities, and astronomy clubs. Many have open evenings when you can visit and use telescopes to view the space objects visible from where you live.

ONLINE

Canadian Space Agency
www.asc-csa.gc.ca/eng/satellites/cubesat/default.asp
Learn about a tiny cube-shaped satellite designed by the Canadian Space Agency and used around the world—and even around Mars!

Cosmoquest
https://cosmoquest.org/
Cosmoquest lets you take part in real projects to map objects in the solar system including the moon, Mars, and Mercury. It is run by NASA and needs the expertise of humans to identify features that can't always be picked out reliably by computers.

Galaxy Zoo
www.galaxyzoo.org
Galaxy Zoo is an international project to classify the shapes of galaxies working from photographs taken by some of the most powerful telescopes in the world. It is available in many languages, including English and Spanish.

The Planetary Society
www.planetary.org
The Planetary Society is the world's largest nonprofit space organization, with more than 50,000 members in 100 countries. On the website, you can take part in citizen-science projects, read about discoveries made by citizen scientists and professional astronomers, and keep up-to-date with astronomy news.

GLOSSARY

analysis Detailed examination of artifacts or data

asteroid A lump of rock, metal, or ice traveling through space, and measuring more than a meter wide

astrophysics The study of the physics that relates to stars, planets, and other objects in space

atmosphere The layer of gases that surrounds a planet

collaborating Working together cooperatively and sharing information

comet A lump of ice and dust that orbits the Sun and is seen in the sky as a bright spot of light trailing a long tail

conference A gathering at which experts discuss their work and share ideas and results

constellation A group of stars that form a recognizable pattern

electromagnetic radiation Waves of energy of different wavelengths with different properties, including visible light, radio, microwaves, and X-rays

evidence Proven facts that show that a hypothesis may be true

exoplanet A planet outside our solar system, usually orbiting another star

fraud Deliberate cheating, lying, or falsifying of results

galaxy A massive collection of stars

gravity The force that acts between bodies that have mass, pulling them together

hypothesis A suggested idea of how something might work or what might happen that has to be stated in terms that can be tested

interpreting The act of figuring out what something means

journal A type of magazine that prints research findings and ideas relating to a particular area of a subject

lander A vehicle that is sent through space to land on another planet, moon, or other object

lensmaker A person who makes lenses, shaped pieces of glass that bend light rays. Lenses are used in telescopes and microscopes to show more detail of distant or very small objects.

light pollution Excess light from street lighting, traffic, and buildings that illuminates the sky

mass A measure of the amount of material that something contains; measured by scientists in grams and kilograms

meteoroid A small lump of rock or metal traveling through space, and measuring less than a meter wide

microwaves Waves of electromagnetic radiation that can be used to heat up food or carry communications signals

model An object or image used to show or explain an idea

observatory A site where astronomers make observations of space using telescopes or other instruments

orbit The circular or elliptical path of one object around another

planetarium A theater for showing displays about space, often using a dome-shaped overhead screen onto which images of stars and planets are projected

probe A remotely controlled space vehicle sent to gather data or samples from somewhere in space

radio waves Electromagnetic radiation with a long wavelength that can be detected and examined to provide information about large astronomical objects

rover A remotely controlled vehicle for traveling over the surface of a moon, another planet, an asteroid, or comet to collect data and sometimes samples

satellite An object that is in orbit around a moon, planet, or star

solar system A star and the planets, moons, comets, and other objects in orbit around it

taxes Money paid by people to the government to fund large public projects such as the police, road-building, and education

USSR Former Union of Soviet Socialist Republics centered around Russia that was disbanded in the 1990s, after which many of the countries became independent

X-rays Waves of electromagnetic radiation with a very short wavelength that can travel through some materials but are stopped by very dense materials, including metal and bone

INDEX

ABOUT THE AUTHOR

Anne Rooney is a full-time writer, specializing in books on science and the history of science for young people and adults. She has written several books on astronomy, including *Space Record Breakers* and the *Stars and Planets Handbook* for young people, and *The Story of Astronomy* and *Mapping the Universe* for adults.